The Essential James Reaney

The Essential James Reaney

selected by Brian Bartlett

The Porcupine's Quill

Library and Archives Canada Cataloguing in Publication

Reaney, James, 1926–2008
The essential James Reaney / selected by Brian Bartlett.

(Essential poets ; 4)
Poems.
ISBN 978-0-88984-319-6

I. Bartlett, Brian, 1953– II. Title.
III. Series: Essential poets (Erin, Ont.) ; 4

PS8535.E24A6 2009a C811'.54 C2009-903843-9

1 2 3 4 • 12 11 10 09

Published by The Porcupine's Quill, 68 Main Street, PO Box 160,
Erin, Ontario N0B 1T0. http://porcupinesquill.ca

Interior illustrations (with the exception of page three) are by James Reaney.

Represented in Canada by the Literary Press Group.
Trade orders are available from University of Toronto Press.

We acknowledge the support of the Ontario Arts Council and the Canada Council for the Arts for our publishing program. The financial support of the Government of Canada through the Book Publishing Industry Development Program is also gratefully acknowledged. Thanks, also, to the Government of Ontario through the Ontario Media Development Corporation's Ontario Book Initiative.

Canada

ONTARIO ARTS COUNCIL
CONSEIL DES ARTS DE L'ONTARIO

Canada Council for the Arts
Conseil des Arts du Canada

Table of Contents

Foreword

One evening in the late 1940s, the poet Earle Birney went to a party and met an undergraduate over twenty years younger than himself. Much later he would recall that stranger: '... a small packet of firecrackers set alight, he went sizzling and leaping mischievously from one guest to another, an excited child popping adult questions, bounding into the kitchen and back to the hall, and continually exploding with ideas, images and emotions. I thought him a marvellously inventive Ariel, and still do.' That young stranger, James Reaney, would soon win the Governor General's Award in 1949 when he was only twenty-three years old, for his first collection of poems, *The Red Heart*. Much of the subsequent commentary on that book referred to its darkness, its glimpses of stunted childhoods and embittering communities, but Birney's image of Reaney as Ariel is valuable, since the book is leavened with tonal lightness, delight in metaphor and odd detail, and spirited inventiveness. Despite his deserved reputation as the father of Southwestern Ontario Gothic, Reaney was one of the most playful and buoyant of Canadian poets publishing in the 1940s and '50s. The mixture of disturbing grotesquery and entertaining whimsy in his poems is, I hope, amply embodied in the following selection.

The flexibility of Reaney's poetry is shown in its range of voices. He has poems that address a dog, the Avon River, God, the Muse of Satire, downstairs furniture, and the to-be-resurrected dead; poems in the voices of Lake Superior, a lonely child on a farm, Death, a nasty ghost, and geese named Branwell and Lobo. His omnivorous imagination is also evident in its range of allusions and references, from Isaiah, Shakespeare, and Emily Brontë to the Katzenjammer Kids and Rin-Tin-Tin, from Egyptian hieroglyphics and Penelope's fingers to the Orange Lodge, zeppelins, and Ernie's Barber Salon. Reaney's language itself often pushes back against the restraints and oppressions of a culture the poems satirize. His poems inhabit what a late work of his referred to as 'a tavern called the Noun. / And a gymnasium called the Verb'. His diction is often built upon familiar and common words, but also dips into the likes of 'sardonyx', 'chalcedony', and 'idlurious', or comes up with coinings like 'Godwanaland', 'heartsmith', and 'tricklerain'. Against the spectres of solitude and death, Reaney pits his lively rhythms and seductive sounds. 'The Plum Tree' evokes the plight of a farm boy trapped in loneliness and profound silence, where plums 'are like blue pendulums / That thrum the gold-wired winds of summer. / In the opium-still noon they hang or fall, / The plump, ripe plums.' Not only the plums' Keatsian sensuousness but also the 'um's of those lines – plum, pendulum, thrum, summer, opium, plump – suggest a mantric life force beneath the grimness of the environment. A tension between the threat of morbidity and an expressive freedom is often felt in Reaney's earlier poems.

In the first fifteen years or so of Reaney's poem-making, death and childhood are pervasive – not that these themes vanished after 1960: his sequence *The Dance of Death at London, Ontario* was published in 1963. Whether Reaney writes of a carrion bird called 'Devouring Years', or – in 'Dark Lagoon', a masterly poem of prenatal fatedness – of death prophesied for every infant, his poetry is shaded with the implacable course of mortality. Yet the poems are rarely lugubrious in tone; a madcap intelligence is never far away. Children appear often in the poems, nowhere more freshly or unusually than in 'Antichrist as a Child' (an early, less successful version of that poem was in the first person, spoken by the Antichrist himself); there the child seems perplexed and passive, a victim of compulsions he doesn't understand rather than a manipulator or strategist. In other poems we find a 'low I.Q. farmboy' whose head spins with 'Vast God and the interiors of tree trunks', a baby who was 'an old man one hour old', and an adolescent cycling to school 'murmuring irregular verbs'. Reaney's attraction to childhood as a field for poetry is rooted in his youth as an only child in rural Ontario, the first breeding ground for his sense of both suffering and joy, providing what his later friend the musician John Beckwith called 'a whole world of wonderful images coming out of that grain of sand that is the farm' (spoken in Mark McCurdy's and Nancy Johnson's documentary film *James Reaney: Listening to the Wind*).

If Reaney's poems depict the stultifying effects of environment, they find in metaphor, symbolism and audacious imagination not only ways of expressing threats and terrors to human sanity and health but also the pleasures of poetry and other kinds of creativity. In the McCurdy/Johnson film, Reaney says that his favourite course-evaluation comment among those he received for his teaching was 'Dr Reaney exaggerates' ('I'm going to have that put on my tombstone'). In the film he also speaks of his homeland's attitude to the mind-expanding exaggerations of myth: 'The immediate response on the part of Southwestern Ontario is that "I don't want to believe in anything before breakfast – especially if it's impossible."' But 'the impossible' often serves as Reaney's bread and butter. To him a record-player can be a 'beastly bird' on a bank by 'the lake / At Gramaphone'; Death tells a poet, 'All your tropes and iambics / Become my leaden fiddlesticks'; and a huge fan appears in the sky, tremendous enough to 'blow giants & battlefields like dead leaves away'. However, if fancifulness were all, Reaney's inventions might wear on us and show the strains of too much cleverness. Instead, they co-exist with sharp social observations and views of community. 'Klaxon' is a comic poem about a town's obsession with cars, which become personified in the poet's imagination; and 'Shakespearean Gardens' is a multi-part prose-poem that finds Shakespearean parallels in Stratford, Ontario, in a thunderstorm, a lumber-yard accident, a school and a boarding house. Reaney's *A Suit of Nettles*, a form-switching, book-length satire inspired by Renaissance poet Edmund Spenser's *Shepheardes Calendar*, takes on several targets (education, religion, literary criticism) within the fantasy of competing, loving, speaking geese. Some of this book's earlier readers found it a disappointing retreat into bookishness and pastiche after *The Red Heart*, but in retrospect it emerges as Reaney's finest extended achievement in poetry, including passages of his sweetest lyricism and his most piercing, perennially apt satire.

A more comprehensive study of Reaney than I can give here would look at the intersections between his poetry and his plays. For the most part, the latter dominated his writing for the last several decades of his life. All I'll point out is that two of the poems in this Porcupine's Quill selection reappeared, after their first publications, as passages in Reaney's *One-man Masque*, which he performed on stage several times in 1960, and which impressed and astonished a young student named Margaret Atwood. Readers of *The Essential James Reaney* might enjoy knowing that stage directions in *One-man Masque* indicate that 'The Ghost' is spoken after the actor 'draws on huge brown furry motoring gloves', and that in its theatrical context

'Doomsday, or The Red Headed Woodpecker' – Reaney at his most delightfully exclamatory and gusto-driven – is to be yelled through a megaphone.

Reaney's influence on Canadian poetry has not yet been recognized adequately. His humour is surely echoed at times in the poetry of another long-time resident of Southwestern Ontario, Don McKay, who not so coincidentally was once Reaney's student. Reaney's dictionary-ransacking wordplay in a poem like 'The Alphabet' caught the attention of bpNichol, who once wrote that Reaney was 'an explorer & an innovator ... obsessed with language and sound'. And its form-jumping, community-exploring, Gothic-and-Bible-tinged elements, along with the poet's writing for theatre and opera, foreshadow the work of George Elliott Clarke. The title *The Essential James Reaney* may be something of a misnomer, since the essential Reaney includes, besides poetry, a fervent engagement with playwriting and theatre, as well as experiments in short fiction, writing for children and painting. But even by themselves, the poems in this selection give us the unforgettable experience of an imagination that is both shape-giving and – in the final word of one of Reaney's earliest poems – 'overflowing'.

– BRIAN BARTLETT

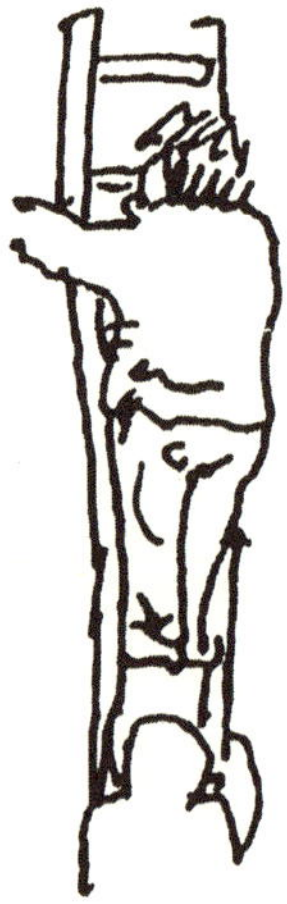

The Antiquary

Within these jars and casks
I keep French and German moonlight
And that variety
That falls on the fieldish mouse
Crossing the floor of a farmer's kitchen.
I have chests of castles leprosied
By wind and by rain
Where young knights sigh
In iron purses.
Here are Wordsworth's vegetables
That teach a nobler life.
Here in these flasks
Lie the coughs of Emily Brontë,
The urine of Dr John Donne,
And Jane Austen's caul.
Here is Queen Anne's seventh child
Pickled in liquor ...

A Prayer

Water obeys the rules set down
Of creeks and rivers, oceans and fountains
Of china and glass and crockery
But I, O Lord, only Thy Dish
In which you apparently placed me;
A Dish of Desires. Which are
Gold wallpaper, cake and tea
Someone playing or singing
An Oboe
Or a Banjo
A white-toothed piano.
Die for me if you must, dear God
But please keep these things overflowing.

The Gramaphone

Upon the lake
At Gramaphone
A beastly bird
Sits on the bank
And dips its beak
Of sharpened bone
Into a haunted
Tank
That ripples with an eternal stone.

When the ladies descend the stairs,
Some eat their fans
And others comb their hair.
But Miss Mumblecrust
Picks up that beastly bird
And dips its beak
Into that round lake
That ripples with eternal stone
And dips its beak of sharpened bone
Into a pool of a young man singing
'I'm all alone
By the telephone!'

Antichrist as a Child

When Antichrist was a child
He caught himself tracing
The capital letter A
On a window sill
And wondered why
Because his name contained no A.
And as he crookedly stood
In his mother's flower-garden
He wondered why she looked so sadly
Out of an upstairs window at him.
He wondered why his father stared so
Whenever he saw his little son
Walking in his soot-coloured suit.
He wondered why the flowers
And even the ugliest weeds
Avoided his fingers and his touch.
And when his shoes began to hurt
Because his feet were becoming hooves
He did not let on to anyone
For fear they would shoot him for a monster.
He wondered why he more and more
Dreamed of eclipses of the sun,
Of sunsets, ruined towns and zeppelins,
And especially inverted, upside down steeples.

Dark Lagoon

Here lies the newborn child
Who, lately, lay within his mother
And stood beside a dark lagoon
Beneath a sunless, starless sky.
Great trees of thick foliage and stout trunks
Hid someone who, far away,
Seemed to be knocking out this epitaph
With muffled chisel on muffled stone:
'This child will someday die.'
But these sounds came really
From his secret Sun,
His mother's heart that hung
Unseen in that dark sky.
The heart, whose tick-tocking
Was life to him, still prophesied
The ticking chisel of the monument-maker
As it should someday carve his name.
His mother's heart, the reason for his being,
Was yet the first clock he ever heard.

Here lies the baby innocent.
He is hardly as large
As the Gettysburg Address
And has never heard
The cry of 'Eenie, meenie, minie, moe',
By which children choose a loser in a game,
And by which Fate seems to choose
Which children shall be which:
One-eyed, wilful, hare-lipped, lame,
Poor, orphans, idiots, or rich.
Nor has he read stories where
People cry, 'I
Am betrayed'; a notion
That shall haunt him all his life
As also shall that dark lagoon
Where once he stood

And seemed in a grave
Though he had not yet been born;
And seemed to hear his mother's heart
Though also a clock
That with little clicking mouthfuls
Began to eat his time.

The Chough

The chough, said a dictionary,
Is a relation of the raven
And a relative of the crow.
It's nearly extinct,
But lingers yet
In the forests of Oporto.
So read I as a little child
And saw a young chough in its nest,
Its very yellow beak already tasting
The delicious eyes
Of missionaries and dead soldiers;
Its wicked mind already thinking
Of how it would line its frowsy nest
With the gold fillings of dead men's teeth.
When I grew older I learned
That the chough, the raven and the crow
That rise like a key signature of black sharps
In the staves and music of a scarlet sunset
Are not to be feared so much
As that carrion bird, within the brain,
Whose name is Devouring Years,
Who gobbles up and rends
All odds and ends
Of memory, good thoughts and recollections
That one has stored up between one's ears
And whose feet come out round either eye.

The Plum Tree

The plums are like blue pendulums
That thrum the gold-wired winds of summer.
In the opium-still noon they hang or fall,
The plump, ripe plums.
I suppose my little sister died
Dreaming of looking up at them,
Of lying beneath that crooked plum tree,
That green heaven with blue stars pied.
In this lonely haunted farmhouse
All things are voiceless save the sound
Of some plums falling through the summer air
Straight to the ground.
And there is no listener, no hearer
For the small thunders of their falling
(Falling as dead stars rush to a winter sea)
Save a child who, lolling
Among the trunks and old featherticks
That fill up the room where he was born,
Hears them in his silent dreaming
On a dark engraving to a fairy-tale forlorn.
Only he hears their intermittent soft tattoo
Upon the dry, brown summer ground
At the edge of the old orchard.
Only he hears, and farther away,
Some happy animal's slow, listless moo.

The Sundogs

I saw the sundogs barking
On either side of the Sun
And he was making his usual will
And last testament
In a glorious vestment.
And the sundogs cried,
'Bow wow!
We'll make a ring
Around the moon
And children, seeing it, will say:
Up there they play Farmer in the Dell
And the moon like the cheese stands still.
Bow wow!
We shall drown the crickets,
Set the killdeer birds crying,
Send shingles flying.
And pick all the apples
Ripe or not.
Our barking shall overturn
Hencoops and rabbit-hutches,
Shall topple over privies
With people inside them,
And burn with invisible,
Oh, very invisible!
Flames
In each frightened tree.
Whole branches we'll bite off
And for the housewife's sloth
In not taking them in
We'll drag her sheets and pillow cases
Off the fence
And dress up in them
And wear them thin.
And people will say
Both in the country
And in the town

It falls in pails
Of iron nails.
We'll blow the curses
Right back into the farmer's mouths
As they curse our industry
And shake their fists,
For we will press the oats
Close to the ground,
Lodge the barley,
And rip open the wheat stooks.
We shall make great faces
Of dampness appear on ceilings
And blow down chimneys
Till the fire's lame.
With the noise of a thousand typewriters
We shall gallop over the roofs of town.
We are the Sun's animals.
We stand by him in the West
And ready to obey
His most auburn wish
For Rain, Wind and Storm.'

The Katzenjammer Kids

With porcupine locks
And faces which, when
More closely examined,
Are composed of measle-pink specks,
These two dwarf imps,
The Katzenjammer Kids,
Flitter through their Desert Island world.
Sometimes they get so out of hand
That a blue Captain
With stiff whiskers of black wicker
And an orange Inspector
With a black telescope
Pursue them to spank them
All through that land
Where cannibals cut out of brown paper
In cardboard jungles feast and caper,
Where the sea's sharp waves continually
Waver against the shore faithfully
And the yellow sun above is thin and flat
With a collar of black spikes and spines
To tell the innocent childish heart that
It shines
And warms (see where she stands and stammers)
The dear fat mother of the Katzenjammers.
Oh, for years and years she has stood
At the window and kept fairly good
Guard over the fat pies that she bakes
For her two children, these dancing heartaches.
Oh, the blue skies of that funny paper weather!
The distant birds like two eyebrows close together!
And the rustling paper roar
Of the waves
Against the paper sands of the paper shore!

Klaxon

All day cars mooed and shrieked,
Hollered and bellowed and wept
Upon the road.
They slid by with bits of fur attached,
Fox-tails and rabbit-legs,
The skulls and horns of deer,
Cars with yellow spectacles
Or motorcycle monocle,
Cars whose gold eyes burnt
With a too-rich battery,
Murderous cars and manslaughter cars,
Chariots from whose foreheads leapt
Silver women of ardent bosom.
Ownerless, passengerless, driverless,
They came to anyone
And with headlights full of tears
Begged for a master,
For someone to drive them
For the familiar chauffeur.
Limousines covered with pink slime
Of children's blood
Turned into the open fields
And fell over into ditches,
The wheels kicking helplessly.
Taxis begged trees to step inside
Automobiles begged of posts
The whereabouts of their mother.
But no one wished to own them any more,
Everyone wished to walk.

Lake Superior

I am Lake Superior
Cold and gray.
I have no superior;
All other lakes
Haven't got what it takes;
All are inferior.
I am Lake Superior
Cold and gray.
I am so cold
That because I chill them
The girls of Fort William
Can't swim in me.
I am so deep
That when people drown in me
Their relatives weep
For they'll never find them.
In me swims the fearsome
Great big sturgeon.
My shores are made of iron
Lined with tough, wizened trees.
No knife of a surgeon
Is sharper than these
Waves of mine
That glitter and shine
In the light of the Moon, my mother
In the light of the Sun, my grandmother.

The Ghost

The evening waddles over the fields like a turkey.
I lurk,
Where my knowledge was chopped from my power.
All knowledge waits for you at the corner here so murky.

The awkward doltish low I.Q. farmboy shambles down the steps,
The empty echoing pitcher in his hand:
I am!
Ha ha! And his hair stands straight up like brambles.

Everything – Egyptian hieroglyphs and crystallography,
Diary of shadows,
Vast God and the interiors of tree trunks, snowflakes
All spin like a fiery corkscrew into his psychology.

For I know everything now having passed into source,
Even
Through me he knows himself – a kidnapped prince.
It is too much for him – he falls down – hoarse
As they shriek and lift him up – I am not.

The evening waddles over the fields like a turkey.
I lurk
Where my knowledge was severed from my power.
All knowledge waits for you at the corner here so murky.

The Baby

Small babe, tell me
    As you sit in your mother's cave
What did you build there,
    Little baby mine?

Sir, I made the tooth
    I invented the eye
I played out hair on a comb harp
    I thought up the sigh.

I pounded the darkness to
    Guts, Heart and Head:
America, Eurasia and Africa
    I out of chaos led.

I fought the goblins
    For the heart;
'Twas a jewel they desired,
    But I held it.

I fought off the rats
    From the guts
They nibbled but I
    Smashed the mutts.

I choked the bat so intent
    For the diamond of my mind;
I caught him in the ogre's cellar
    The tub of blood behind.

And the darkness gave me
    Two boneless wands or swords:
I knew not their meaning then
    Whether traps or rewards.

One was the vorpal phallus
    Filled with jostling army,

Henhouse and palace
        Street crowds and history.

Two was the magic tongue
        Stuffed with names and numbers,
The string of song,
        The waker from fallen slumbers.

My mother opened her grave,
        I sprang out a giant
Into another cave
        Where I was a seed again.

Helpless and wriggly small
        As in my father's groin;
My Shakespeare's tongue a wawl
        And impotent my loin.

The sun-egg I must reach
        Was steeples far away,
The world that I must name
        Was shapeless, sneaky gray.

Is it wonder then I rage
        An old man one hour old,
A bridegroom come to a bride
        Careless unready and cold.

My wedding cake's still in the field
        My bride is ninety and maggoty;
My groomsmen glaring hangmen;
        My bridal bed bouldery.

Small babe, tell me
        As you sit in your mother's cave
What do you build there,
        Little baby mine?

The Windyard

I built a windyard for the wind;
    The wind like a wild vast dog came up
To play with weathervanes and corners
    My keyholes and my chinks.

And for the sea I built a well;
    The brookish tomcat gurgled in,
Waterfell and sprung about
    Hunting throats and boots.

I stood a house up for the earth;
    The mappy girl came in
With rut and footstep path
    That wind the traveller up.

A stove I hammered for the sun;
    In flew the golden oriole
To crackle sticks of time
    And sing the loaves of space.

Come girl well yard and stove,
    Come Flesh Heart Mind and Lyre,
Come Earth Water Wind and Fire.
        Well, when they came
Barking, meowing, talking and caroling,
I stepped above both house and yard
        Into myself.

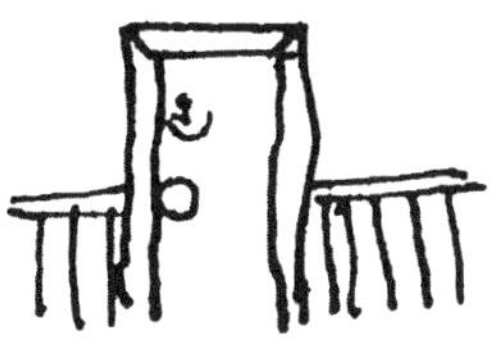

Doomsday, or the Red Headed Woodpecker

I

Red Sky!
Morning!
Shaking like a scarlet head!
Doomsday!
Rise up!
Spring your lids, you dead!
Scrape out
Coffins!
Put yourself together!
Pat that dust!
Find that bust!
This is the last weather!
Trumpet!
Drummer!
Thunder!
Vomit you cannibals!
Shake out those
Those old flesh dresses
For the resurrection parties and balls!

II

Here comes St. Sebastian with a handful of arrows!
The big threshing woodpecker is
Beating on the green drum!
Here comes the poor boy who got caught in the harrows!
Here comes St. Bartholemew with his skin!
Scroll away!
Hell this way!
Heaven that!
Rat a tat tat!
There does Death and there goes Sin!
Here come Cain and Abel
Hand in hand!

Here come horizontals pursued by slopes,
Here comes a table
Changing back to a tree and
Here come the hanged people skipping with their ropes!

III

Red Sky!
Morning!
Shaking like a scarlet head!
Doomsday!
Rise up!
Spring your lids, you dead!
Scrape out
Coffins!
Put yourself together!
Pat that dust!
Find that bust!
This is the last weather!
Trumpet!
Drummer!
Thunder!
Vomit you cannibals!
Shake out those
Those old flesh dresses
For the resurrection parties and balls!

Invocation to the Muse of Satire

With Punch's stick (he holds it in his hand)
Beat fertility into a sterile land,
With hands of hawthorn branches in the winter,
And teeth of cold March rain that bite the soft snow,
And bristly porcupines on which the hunter sits for hair;
With skin of mildew and botfly holes poked through
In hide of long impounded, ancient cow,
With eyes whose tears have quotaed out to ice long ago,
Eyes bright as the critical light upon the white snow;
With arms of gallows wood beneath the bark
And torso made of a million hooked unhooking things,
And legs of stainless steel, knives & scythes bunched together,
And feet with harrows, and with discs for shoes –
Speak, Muse of Satire, to this broken pen
And from its blots and dribbling letter-strings
Unloose upon our farm & barnyard – medicine.

With those feet, dance upon their toes
With those legs, grasp them lovingly about the thighs
With that torso, press against their breasts
With those arms, hug them black and blue
With those eyes, look at them you love
With that cheek, rub against their cheeks
With that hair, put your head down in their laps
With those teeth, give forth playful bites
And shake their hands with hour-long explorations
Of their life and heart and mind-line,
But with that stick of which new ones spring ever
From that vine where it was barbarously cut off,
Beat them about the ears and the four senses
Until, like criminals lashed in famine time,
They bring forth something; until thy goad
Grows so warm it bursts into blossoms.

Here, lady, almost blind with seeing too much
Here is the land with spires and chimneys prickly,
Here is the east of the board and here the west,
Here may you enter and there, before you depart,
May you make the sky red with doom and axey wrath.

Has no one seen the country where your cure has nursed?
It is a land of upturned privies with occupants inside them
Crawling out through new tops like astonished moths
Bursting from their unusual, foul and dark cocoons.

from January

BRANWELL

But is this light, my dear friend Mopso,
That never falls on darkness but between
The nine sick planets would to nothing go?
Can I desire one whit of world I've seen
Displayed in your cartography of spleen?
I shiver at its top, that round cold sea.
Without some isle a sea's a dismal scene.
The world's hot middle where it's he and she
Has grown for me feverish stinging clothes.
Your favourite land is better I agree –
What a round concrete continent of snows!
But too round and too continent for me
For I want offspring summerson autumnman wintersage
And tricklerain thawwind panetap upleaf windrage
Plow and seed and hoe, green, sucklepig, yellowripe,
sicklestraw and all such glamourie.

from June

BRANWELL

I am like a hollow tree
Where the owl & weasel hide
I am like a hollow tree
Dead in the forest of his brothers.

My feet are sensitive as brains
Put hats upon them
My feet are sensitive as brains
All the ground is grassed with knives.

These fingers that once played
Nimbly the harp
These fingers that once played
Are soft & suck as leeches.

My throat where once a song
Flew out like a golden bird
My throat where once a song
Is a woodpecker's bitten door.

My eyes are the entrances
To the kingfishers' nests
My eyes are the entrances
Tunnels of clay lined with fish bones.

I see the red sun sink
For the last time this far north.
The full moon rises: my thoughts fly forth.
Leap forth, oh bird of prey & turncoat ermine,
Nebula out of my mind
That swampy fair
Where the bittern pumps from its cistern of despair.

from August

LOBO

Go bid the soldiers shoot
Go bid each screech owl hoot
For Scrutumnus he is dead
Who contained in his wee head
A sharper sense of good and bad
Than all the ages' gooses had.

BLOT

Go bid the women shriek and cry.
Go bid them black their dresses dye.
He who first showed how to choose
Between the fast, between the loose,
The connoisseur of crickets' songs
Who knew his harps and knew his gongs
Died ere his precious work was done.
Died and veiled with tar our sun.

BUSTO

The song of gull and hawk and shrike
He first discovered, first did like.
The fancy wren, the too sweet lark
He bravely thrust down into dark.
The language of the common sparrow,
The music of the untaught farrow
Held he sweeter far than thrushes
Whistling silver trills and rushes.
Pigs and sparrows sing 'We copulate,'
And mean exactly what they state.

RAYMOND

Egad! Who was this Tamburlaine,
Who said bluebirds sing like a chilblain
And made old reputations fall
Like feathery snow from Mother Holl.

LOBO

Scrutumnus! Scrutumnus! Scrutumnus!
We lay this wreath on thy tumulus!
A wreath of thy favourite pigsweed
And lambsquarters gone to seed.
Bring on the songs and we will play
His favourite game upon this day.

BLOT

Ladies and gentlemen, after I've sung
These three songs from my leather lung
Establish a preference among the three,
But evaluate judiciously.

....

Shortly before his death Scrutumnus heard
And judged these songs; the first!
By John Dong he adjudged the first!
The second by Edmund Lily Goose
Comes second! he said he found it loose
With no real emotion urging it on,
The images overdecorous and overdrawn.
The third he found obscure, a farrago
Of bad English and worse Latin lingo,
No real emotion, no language of the people,
Immoral in its basic avoidance of simplicity,
Pompous overblown fantastically ...

TERPSICHORE

But you and Scrutumnus, sir, do not
Understand these songs. One ought
To see that each has a different purpose
And therefore a different word choice,
You do not laugh at a cat or a frog
Because they cannot act like a hog.

BLOT

I do, madam. You are wrong, wench!

LOBO

Who's this skirted lesbian stench?

BUSTO

Take her prisoner! Tie her down.
We'll give her a green gown.
Give me my pruning hook & sword cane.
Now where my shadow falls on this bane
I'll spare, but where it does not fall
I'll cut an offering for his funeral.

RAYMOND

Your shadow is much shorter than her form.

LOBO

Then she must bow to him, for he's the norm.

. . . .

from October

BRANWELL

GREEN grove walk toward me,
    Around me with
        That which
Trembles heartsmith

Currant tinkle bobbob
    Pheasant leap whir
        Squirrel
A pink mushroom, sir!

Little missy white violets

Squirrel corn
Bloodroots
Bossy lost her horn.

As yet not boxes
Gallows
Legs, pulpits
Of trees windblows.

Hollow tree tuwhoos
Come here
Mousie
And robin redbreast dear.

Far away red faraway
Red as fire
A fox
Flash and transpire.

I met a green woman:
Her feet were paths
Her eyes were bunchberries
Her arms elm laths
Her tongue a mushroom
Her teeth white violets
Her nose an owl feather,
Her mouth like cressets.

Did I touch her?
Vanished.
Twang!
Garnisheed

All pulse-wage since
And this place
Holds my heart in a bottle
Of pathpace.

Near Tobermory, Ontario

I look upon a blue cove
In August
With egg pebble beach,
Blue sky & cedar birch sides.

And I look upon the sisters four
Blue sky & blue water
Rock, pebble & earth
And the light I see it with.

Watty Blue has a drowned man
For her heart
And rain for food & wind
To crisp her thoughts with.

Pale Blue Airy has clouds
To mind & winds to sing,
Thunder to say, lightning to do
And birds to hold.

Urtha lumpily clogs
Her clotty feet,
Waves Aaron's Rod & wears
Emeralds in rags.

But Light, you're quite another thing.
Indeterminate,
You hold them all yet let them slip
Into themselves again.

The Alphabet

Where are the fields of dew?
I cannot keep them.
They quip and pun
The rising sun
Who plucks them out of view:
But lay down fire-veined jasper!

For out of my cloudy head
Come Ay Ee I Oh and U,
Five thunders shouted:
Drive in sardonyx!

And Ull Mm Nn Rr and hisSsings
Proclaim huge wings;
Pour in sea-blue sapphires!

Through my bristling hair
Blows Wuh and Yuh
Puh, Buh, Phuh and Vuh,
The humorous air:
Lift up skies of chalcedony!

Huh, Cuh, Guh and Chuh
Grunt like pigs in my acorn mind:
Arrange these emeralds in a meadow!

Come down Tuh, Duh and Thuh!
Consonantly rain
On the windowpane
Of the shrunken house of the heart;
Lift up blood red sardius!

Lift up golden chrysolite!
Juh, Quuh, Zuh and X
Scribble heavens with light,
Steeples take fright.

In my mouth like bread
Stands the shape of this glory;
Consonants and vowels
Repeat the story:
And sea-green beryl is carried up!

The candle tongue in my dark mouth
Is anguished with its sloth
And stung with self-scoff
As my eyes behold this treasure.
Let them bring up topaz now!

Dazzling chrysoprase!
Dewdrops tempt dark wick to sparkle.
Growl Spark! You whelp and cur,
Leap out of tongue kennel
And candle sepulchre.

I faint in the hyacinthine quarries!
My words pursue
Through the forest of time
The fading antlers of this dew.

A B C D E F G H I J K L M
Take captive the sun
Slay the dew quarry
Adam's Eve is morning rib
Bride and bridegroom marry
Still coffin is rocking crib
Tower and well are one
The stone is the wind, the wind is the stone
New Jerusalem
N O P Q R S T U V W X Y Z !

The Bicycle

Halfway between childhood & manhood,
  More than a hoop but never a car,
The bicycle talks gravel and rain pavement
  On the highway where the dead frogs are.

Like sharkfish the cars blur by,
  Filled with the two-backed beast
One dreams of, yet knows not the word for,
  The accumulating sexual yeast.

Past the house where the bees winter,
  I climb on the stairs of my pedals
To school murmuring irregular verbs
  Past the lion with legs like a table's.

Autumn blows the windfalls down
  With a twilight horn of dead leaves.
I pick them up in the fence of November
  And burrs on my sweater sleeves.

Where a secret robin is wintering
  By the lake in the fir grove dark
Through the fresh new snow we stumble
  That Winter has whistled sharp.

The March wind blows me ruts over,
  Puddles past, under red maple buds,
Over culvert of streamling, under
  White clouds and beside bluebirds.

Fireflies tell their blinking player
  Piano hesitant tales
Down at the bridge through the swamp
  Where the ogre clips his rusty nails.

Between the highschool & the farmhouse
    In the country and the town
It was a world of love and of feeling
    Continually floating down

On a soul whose only knowledge
    Was that everything was something,
This was like that, that was like this –
        In short, everything was
    The bicycle of which I sing.

Shakespearean Gardens

The Tempest
The violet lightning of a March thunderstorm glaring the patches of ice still stuck to the streets.

Two Gentlemen of Verona
On Wellington St. an elegant colonel-looking gentleman with waxed white mustachioes that came to tight little points.

Merry Wives of Windsor
The Ladies' Auxiliary of the Orange Lodge marched down the street in white dresses with orange bows on them.

Richard III
At last all the children ran away from home and were brought up by an old spinster who lived down the street.

Henry VIII
Mr. White's second wife was the first Mrs. Brown and the first Mrs. White was the second Mrs. Brown.

Troilus & Cressida
'Well, I haven't been to that old Festival yet but since it began I've had ten different boyfriends.'

Titus Andronicus
Young Mr. Wood to-day lost his right hand in an accident at the lumber yards.

Romeo & Juliet
Romeo & Juliet Streets.

Timon of Athens
Old Miss Shipman lived alone in a weatherbeaten old cottage and could occasionally be seen out on the front lawn cutting the grass with a small sickle.

Julius Caesar
Antony wore a wrist watch in the Normal School production although he never looked at it during the oration.

Macbeth
Principal Burdoch's often expressed opinion was that a great many people would kill a great many other people if they knew for certain they could get away with it.

Hamlet
A girl at the bakery took out a boat on the river, tied candlesticks to her wrists and drowned herself.

King Lear
Mr. Upas was a silver haired cranky old individual who complained that the meat was too tough at the boarding house.

Othello
At the edge of the town stood a lonely white frame building – a deserted Negro church.

The Merchant of Venice
When my cousin worked for the Silversteins she had her own private roll of baloney kept aside in the refrigerator for her.

Henry V
The local armouries are made of the usual red brick with the usual limestone machicolation.

To the Avon River above Stratford, Canada

What did the Indians call you?
For you do not flow
With English accents.
I hardly know
What I should call you
        Because before
I drank coffee or tea
        I drank you
        With my cupped hands
And you did not taste English to me
        And you do not sound
        Like Avon
        Or swans & bards
But rather like the sad wild fowl
        In prints drawn
        By Audubon
And like dear bad poets
        Who wrote
        Early in Canada
And never were of note.
You are the first river
        I crossed
And like the first whirlwind
        The first rainbow
        First snow, first
        Falling star I saw,
You, for other rivers are my law.
        These other rivers:
        The Red & the Thames
        Are never so sweet
To skate upon, swim in
        Or for baptism of sin.
        Silver and light
The sentence of your voice,
        With a soprano
Continuous cry you shall

Always flow
Through my heart.
The rain and the snow of my mind
Shall supply the spring of that river
Forever.
Though not your name
Your coat of arms I know
And motto:
A shield of reeds and cresses
Sedges, crayfishes
The hermaphroditic leech
Minnows, muskrats and farmers' geese
And printed above this shield
One of my earliest wishes
'To flow like you.'

from The Dance of Death at London, Ontario

The Clergyman

PRIEST: I often think as I drink tea
  Of Faith & Hope & Charity.
MINISTER: I'm sure that Faith, Hope & Charity
  Oft think of us as we drink tea.

Death

Shepherds, the morning sky is red.
  I've found half of thy charge.
Whatever thy task was, find it out,
  For I'm near and much at large.

....

The Bride & The Bridegroom

SHE: Mother & father have spared no expense.
  Is that someone's foot on my train?
HE: I bet I remember this moment
  Again & again & again.

Death

There go the bride & the bridegroom!
  They'll stay at our hostelry.
To its luscious bridal chamber
  We've devised an ancient key.

The Child

On Dawnview Ave I live.
  Our sidewalk's just put in.
I play outside till it's Cartoon Time
  Or sometimes Rin-Tin-Tin.

Death

My hoop is Time which I drive on
  Quicker than you can, my boy.
  I drive it down this street to-day
Since you are now my newest toy.

. . . .

The Poet

Since I write you I well know
  What you will doubtless say
That every word I write must go
  The dusty change of vowel way.

Death

Of course. All your tropes and iambics
  Become my leaden fiddlesticks.
My laurel soon will make you dull,
  And your tongue dust pepper in your skull.

from A City in Greenland

[...] But this
Was a metropolis where we were the language
And the words were us.
Every once in a while I feel again
As if a word were trying to speak me,
And I feel myself changing into her
As the subterranean hyphen blurs into a river.

You ask why it is that language works,
And you say that it's because words are the directory,
The outline, the street plan
For a city we once lived in
And will again.
First I was a father's gesture
Accepted by a mother's Noun: Verb copula Noun.
If we talk the right way, we slowly story the city back
And release it from the two-mile prison of snow
That fell on top of it when the cosmic ruffians
Inside our planet rolled over in their sleep
And broke up Godwanaland into four drifting disjuncts.

You delight in the flutter shadows of leaves on pavement?
Those leafshadows are children playing there.
All sounds are the splashing of the Great Spring
Dancing up in their Market Square
Which they bit from, not drank.
Our sight is the tree, the tree that grew there
In whose branches we sing, the nerve ghost tree of blood
And nervous mycellium.
Our taste and smell were street cars and boats.
There was a tavern called the Noun.
And a gymnasium called the Verb.
Banks saved up prepositionings,
Bake shops sold stories you could eat,
And rich skunk histories,
Musk etchings,

Cinnamon in a stout cage
Our touch was the red lighthouse beacon
In a grasshopper's leg
With which we jump over death.
A man, I was the tongue of a woman.
Where is that city now?
Under two miles of historical snow.

....

from Footnotes and Podiatry

3. In the nervous palaces of my labyrinthine mind
        Are neural nebulae,
   Bigger than the one we think's outside of us.

   I wonder is there a difference
   Between where the fingers live
   And the toes live?
   One a house, one a stable?
   Penelope's fingers wove, her toes treadled the loom.
   Krishna dances while he plays the flute,
   Makes love as well, to bring in another foot!
        I see them at night
        Asleep in their gloves
          and their spats beds,
   One dancer wakes up, conscious for his shoe.

7. Street
   Speak
   Feet
   Speak
   Street

21. Cows with their independent toes
Of horn & cud philosophy
Write primitive sentences
Make their very own paths!
By no means as straight as Roma's
or the Lord's in Isaiah,
Or the surveyors of Canada Upper
Who followed the stars' whatever.

24. Bare feet speak a flop drip sea-dialect
Not the tough pen nib of cowhide copperplate.

26. Feet are handles in exile,
Condemned to work in axle
In mere travel
When they would so much rather
Have preferred to play the piano.

30. Ah, the differing sounds high heels make
I thought when sloppily my street
Found a horsey voice of frail miss
In recently bought Clydesdale-sounding
High-heeled Bata clompers.

Paths & roads
Are the stories & odes
Of our legs, ankles, soles & toes.

My mother when uptown to
Market also bought
A special kind of
Powder to stop
The incessant creaking of a new
Shoe,

Everyone's feet
Speak an ideodialect.

The Fan

A girl spent all day pleating a fan.
Either we have Verdun & Kursk
Or we have herbivorous people
As the she above
Who spend all day in their garden
Watching butterflies
Or playing with a kite
Or cutting out coloured paper
For a fan
Or a kite
Or balancing the reds of zinnias with those of
amaranths,
For example that plant called Love Lies Bleeding.

I saw a field of men playing football
With a criminal's head.
I saw a field of sunflowers wiped out
By ten thousand tanks.
I saw Aunt Marjorie's paint brush
Destroy a knight in armour
And even a villainous peasant!
I saw our hockey player break a Russian player's
ankle!

And I saw the Fan! giant in the sky
Huge, winnowing!
I saw an armoured car drive up
To arrest an artist
Who was accounted hopelessly a- and un-political
Because he painted nothing but flowers & mice,
But of course he was suddenly seen
As the most dangerous rebel in the republic.
And I saw the Fan – big, winnowing,
Make a rhapsody of a windy day,
Separate wheat from straw just like that,
And blow giants & battlefields like dead leaves away!

The Duck

I

Green grass & white duck,
Orange & yellow beak,
Orange & yellow feet.
White stands out plump!
Quack! in the fresh brown pond.
Heads down now in underwater castle!
Up now! floating with duckling passel.
Floating Simpletons,
In Air Court, Water Castle, Sun Ladder,
Please! Surround me with your vision.

II

By the river, just above the dam,
In front of the public changing rooms,
And a beach brought from a kame,

A crowd of grassy idlurious are standing
Watching thro' average secular prisms
Our Evangelical Church's baptisms.

Still in his shoes & his best suit,
Reverend McLeod
Steps into the river.

Come now his would-be followers
Of Jesus: in their best clothes –
White shirts, white shoes, white dresses,

Burgers & burgesses burgeoning last progresses
Of Pilgrim's Progress into Jordan
In their minister's New Jerusalarms.

They reply to his query, 'Yes, an orange Yes!'

And he dips them down
While the whole town
Stands curiously dry.

Let us take St. Paul at his word
When he compares Noah's Ark to baptism.

Look at that large working duck-man;
He tars his bottom
He draws up his drawbridge,
Shingles his hair against the long rain,
And dives into the arms of his minister
Like a good monster, into the grip
Of Reverend McLeod, who holds him under
For a forty day water trip.

Down in Water Castle he's concentrating
And jammy crystallizing
All his two-by-two heart, thought, & flesh
Animals!
Such as the tigers of procreation, the elephants
Of work, the hippopotamus of birth,
The dove of life, the raven of death.

Afterwards, in the sun-laddered bath house,
Taking off his wet, puddly clothes,
He seems an ordinary man.
I can see he was born, I see he will die.
He can, & has, reproduced himself, he can
Produce himself, but then I see

He's not a man, but a babe in a new world
Whose tiger hills chaos not just red blubber,
Whose river-horse is a bouncing ball,
Not a monster; whose elephant plays,
Not drudges; whose raven will never

Come back; whose dove carries back the twig of Life,
And whose head is a round rainbow.

O floating, naked simpleton,
Ridiculously pure,
Dock now thy rainboat,
You baptized Jordan swimmer,
Dock it now on my Armenian mountain head,
Ararat!
So I beneath you
May *understand* thee!

'White Grumphies, white snow ...'

The students of Agricultural Diploma, their fathers
Grow square miles of blue flowering flax near
Pilot Mound and square miles of yellow mustard which
I saw as I drove out from Minnesota,
Well knowing that in the fall, in the autumn,
We would be teaching them Robert Penn Warren's
Understanding Poetry, Austen's *Pride and Prejudice*,
Somerset Maugham, Joseph Conrad, Emily Dickinson.

As I climbed the stairs to their classroom
Over the Rupertsland Agricultural Auditorium,
Prepared to teach them 'I heard a fly buzz when I died',
I heard them splitting desk into kindling
For a bonfire in a waste paper basket where they
Burnt the texts on the course one by one.
Rainbow-coloured poems and prose they burnt,
Book by book, as I taught them.
As verbal virgins they were tougher
Than such pastoral nymphs as Diana or urban ones
Such as Athena.

However, a day or two later, taking a random stroll
Across the winter campus, I saw
Around the corner of the Swine Barn, a herd
Of white, white pigs being driven into the barn
By my Aggie Dip students each with
A very proper and even beautiful pig-driving stick.
Was it their mid-term test in pig herding?
It must have been.
The whiteness of the piggies against the whiteness of the snow
Presented them with optical problems.
They had trouble seeing me as well.
In fact not one of them did, for I
Was wearing this poem.

Don Quixot de la Verismo

Once, *auf Kanada,* I met
A different kind of Don Quixot.
Instead of collecting romances,
He owned several hundreds of realistic novels!
Many copies of James T. Farrell,
And many many copies of Theodore Dreis-
er, illustrated, non-illustrated.
All bought with zeal never sated.
As for Émile Zola – ooh lala, Zoo la la –
His collected works piled on a sofa!

Now this Don Quixot went on a quest
To find nothing of particular interest,
But just to let the environment
Over him be absolutely dominant.
He tried hard not to have adventures,
And talked to people mostly of their dentures.
Until he saw one day
Beside his highway
Giants lined up on the hills.
He thought they were windmills!
And would they grind some flour for him
And fill his water pail to the brim?
Oh, these giants with their giantesses
Of windmills were quite the antitheses.
When he climbed up to them with pail and bag of wheat
Hoping to get something to drink and eat
These giants with terrific ease
Tore him to pieces!
Oh tale of woe!
Another victim of *verismo*!
Don't forget he had a Sancho Panza
Who lagged behind him like a second stanza
And kept telling him they weren't windmills,
'We live in a fairy tale, not in "real-life" novels!
The Brothers Grimm were right

Dreiser, Farrell and Zola ain't!'
Don Quixot's squire scampered off with a wail,
But not without the wheat and the pail,
Deserting this highway for a nearby wood
As fast as he could!

Elderberry Cottage

's windows, last night, rain wrote upon.
And Bobdog, while he slept, was miles away,
Beating the bounds, our frontier nose-spy
Reporting back at dawn.
We reward him for knowing about
Quarrels in lover's lane,
Thieves on the prowl and other such
Nightwalkers.
Canny protector, I pray you:
Bark always when strangers come nigh.
Yes, we cannot smell trespass
Nor hear it, as you can.
Piss a ring of fire round our house,
Our curtilage, my land, my concessional lot.
Lead me safely at last
Under this township to my last cot,
And when Elderberry is a ruin,
Guard my grave from the academic wolf,
The curious professor
With his fine wire-brush
Would dig me up again
From my happiness, your kingdom.

from Brush Strokes Decorating a Fan

(a)
In bed at night
I think of you
Downstairs there
In the dark –
Chair, table, cupboard,
Dishes, books, my outside boots,
Dear good things
That wait
Patient-
ly
All night
For me & the morning.
Still there
When I get up
And come down
To you

(c)
O cloud unreachable in air
O icicle in my gloved hand
O water in your cupped hand

(g)
Ernie's Barber Salon Near the College.
Mr. Delilah, the Barber,
Cuts a field of hair
In his basement shop
When I duck down to see him
In the fraternity field

Scything away

(o)

The ethicals are
Putting on their overshoulds
Picking up their mights
Wandering the woulds
Prowling for cans
And shalls

(p)

Orchard
First a haw,
Small, red, round.
Next a sour
Red & yellow crab.
Then the Ben Davis,
Scarlet, not ripe until March,
But still, even then,
A hog choker
Which you married to Mr. McIntosh
Who smoothed me to the delicious Courtland

(t)

You tore my Jesus from his lake
But put no nymph back,
Only a scum
Petroleum

(v)

The hand of my ear
Picks up a distant bell

(w)

I know a book that opens up people
And reads them,
Spreads them out, pleat by pleat,
Till they see as far up as up,
Till they see farther far than down.
It makes so sharp their eyes
That East or West
They can spot Nobody coming up the Road

(y)

Sick, I came to my sister's abbey for refuge.
My outlaw forest outside her ruled windows.
In white, she now stands over me
Drinking my blood with sharp lancet.
Satisfied, she waits for my finish.
But my horn she has overlooked
Which I blow upon to summon John
Who brings me my great bow.
It defies her with an arrow
Shooting up & far over my forest
To where I must be buried
There to grow again:
New forest, new merry ways, new story

(z)

Up a walk into a house
I ran
They put me in the stove
Out its chimney smoke
I rose
Into Heaven's Love

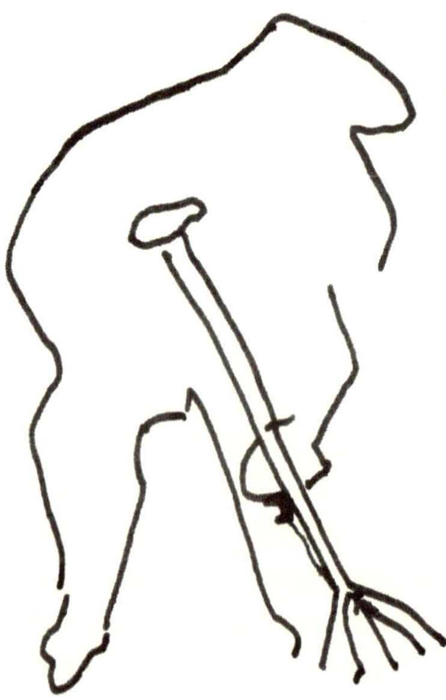

About James Reaney

At James Reaney's funeral in June 2008, his son's tribute recalled the father as many things: poet, playwright, puppeteer, director, painter, historian, regionalist, scholar, student, wit, visionary, patriot, organic farmer, long-distance cyclist, shivaree-maker, dragon-slayer and conversationalist (and that list is incomplete, giving less than half the terms used by Reaney's son). In an energetic life that lasted eighty-two years, James Reaney had a major impact on the people and culture of southwestern Ontario, and that impact has been felt across Canada by those attuned to his poetry, his plays and his other achievements.

Born in 1926 on a farm near Stratford, Ontario, James (Jamie) Crerar Reaney was the only child of James Nesbitt Reaney and Elizabeth (née Crerar) Reaney. His mother's ancestors were Highland Scots; his father's were from Ulster. Once in Ontario, the families were variously Presbyterians, Plymouth Brethren, and Independent Gospel Hallers. Reaney's father suffered from bouts of poor physical and mental health; years later, Reaney recalled how he 'let me moon about the house, read books and practice music'. Reaney went to a one-room school in Elmhurst, Stratford Collegiate and Vocational Institute, and Victoria College at the University of Toronto, achieving some freedom from his evangelical upbringing and receiving a BA in 1948, then an MA the following year. While in Toronto, he gained notoriety for his short story 'The Box-Social', in particular for the image of an aborted fetus. (Though as a student he published several stories in a rural or small-town Gothic vein, these wouldn't be gathered into a book until 1996.) Also in 1949, at the age of twenty-three, he won the first of his three Governor General's Awards, for his first poetry collection, *The Red Heart*, and began to teach English at the University of Manitoba. Two years later he married Colleen Thibaudeau, a former classmate and another poet, who would go on to publish memorable, innovative poetry collections such as *The Martha Landscapes* and *The Artemesia Book*. Their two sons, James and John, were born in 1952 and 1954. During his eleven years based in Manitoba, Reaney took a leave of absence to do a Ph.D. back at the University of Toronto, completing a dissertation, 'The Influence of Spenser on Yeats'. While in Toronto, he finished his satirical and lyrical tour-de-force *A Suit of Nettles*. His and Colleen's daughter, Susan, was born in 1959, the year before the family moved back permanently to Ontario.

The fall he started teaching at the University of Western Ontario – where he remained until his retirement in 1989 – Reaney published the first issue of his magazine *Alphabet: A Semi-Annual Devoted to the Iconography of the Imagination*. As an editor he published poets such as Jay Macpherson, Al Purdy, Milton Acorn, Margaret Atwood and bpNichol. For its eleven-year duration, in its focus on the mythological aspects of literature, the magazine showed the powerful influence of Reaney's teacher and mentor Northrop Frye. Through his teaching career Reaney was also dedicated to the culture and geography of his native region, devising courses such as 'An ABC to Ontario Literature and Culture'. By the early 1960s Reaney was becoming recognized as a librettist (for *Night-Blooming Cereus*, a John Beckwith opera performed on the CBC in 1959) and a playwright, author of *The Killdeer*, *One-man Masque* and *The Sun and the Moon*. Tragedy struck the family in 1966 when Reaney's son John died of meningitis at age twelve.

Later in the decade and for the rest of his life, Reaney's passion for theatre overshadowed his writing of poetry, resulting in many plays such as *Colours in the Dark*, *Listen to the Wind* and, most famously, *The Donnellys*, a non-linear, poetically charged trilogy inspired by a nineteenth-century Ontario Irish family killed by a hostile community. Reaney's later theatrical creations and musical collaborations included two more projects with Beckwith, *The Shivaree* and – including live action and eighteen five-foot-high puppets – *Crazy to Kill: A Detective Opera*; the chamber opera *Serinette*, with music by Harry Somers; and a stage adaptation of Lewis Carroll's *Alice Through the Looking-Glass*. He was a vital, beloved force in theatre workshops and drama productions. His later poetry collections were published in 1990 and 2005. A few months before Reaney's death, the McMichael Canadian Art Collection in Kleinburg, Ontario, mounted a show called 'The Iconography of the Imagination', composed of fifty landscapes, drawings and sketches that Reaney had completed during his creatively rich life.

James Reaney: A Bibliography

POETRY

The Red Heart (1949)
A Suit of Nettles (1958)
Twelve Letters to a Small Town (1962)
The Dance of Death at London, Ontario (1963)
Poems (1972)
Selected Shorter Poems (1975)
Selected Longer Poems (1976)
Imprecations: The Art of Swearing (1984)
Performance Poems (1990)
Souwesto Home (2005)

DRAMA

The Killdeer & Other Plays (1962)
Let's Make a Carol: A Play with Music for Children (1965)
Colours in the Dark (1969)
Listen to the Wind (1972)
Masks of Childhood (1972)
Names & Nicknames and Other Plays for Young People (1972)
Apple Butter and Other Plays for Children (1973)
Baldoon. With C.H. Gervais (1976)
Sticks and Stones: The Donnellys, Part 1 (1976)
The St. Nicholas Hotel: The Donnellys, Part 2 (1976)
Handcuffs: The Donnellys, Part 3 (1977)
The Dismissal; or Twisted Beards and Tangled Whiskers (1978)
Wacousta (1979)
Gyroscope: A New Play (1983)
Crazy to Kill: A Detective Opera (1988)
Lewis Carroll's Alice Through the Looking-Glass. Adapted for Stage (1994)
Two Plays (2003)
Scripts: Librettos for Opera and Other Musical Works (2004)

FICTION & OTHER PROSE

The Boy with an R in His Hand (1965)
14 Barrels from Sea to Sea (1977)
Take the Big Picture (1986)
The Box Social and Other Stories (1996)